YOUR KNOWLEDGE HAS VALUE

- We will publish your bachelor's and master's thesis, essays and papers

- Your own eBook and book - sold worldwide in all relevant shops

- Earn money with each sale

Upload your text at www.GRIN.com
and publish for free

Jon Michael Jachimowicz

Aus der Reihe: e-fellows.net stipendiaten-wissen

e-fellows.net (Hrsg.)

Band 618

Heuristics: a source of judgement fallacies or decision-making aids?

GRIN Verlag

Bibliografische Information der Deutschen Nationalbibliothek:

Die Deutsche Bibliothek verzeichnet diese Publikation in der Deutschen National-bibliografie; detaillierte bibliografische Daten sind im Internet über http://dnb.d-nb.de/ abrufbar.

Dieses Werk sowie alle darin enthaltenen einzelnen Beiträge und Abbildungen sind urheberrechtlich geschützt. Jede Verwertung, die nicht ausdrücklich vom Urheberrechtsschutz zugelassen ist, bedarf der vorherigen Zustimmung des Verlages. Das gilt insbesondere für Vervielfältigungen, Bearbeitungen, Übersetzungen, Mikroverfilmungen, Auswertungen durch Datenbanken und für die Einspeicherung und Verarbeitung in elektronische Systeme. Alle Rechte, auch die des auszugsweisen Nachdrucks, der fotomechanischen Wiedergabe (einschließlich Mikrokopie) sowie der Auswertung durch Datenbanken oder ähnliche Einrichtungen, vorbehalten.

Imprint:

Copyright © 2012 GRIN Verlag GmbH
Druck und Bindung: Books on Demand GmbH, Norderstedt Germany
ISBN: 978-3-656-34642-5

This book at GRIN:

http://www.grin.com/en/e-book/203666/heuristics-a-source-of-judgement-fallacies-or-decision-making-aids

GRIN - Your knowledge has value

Der GRIN Verlag publiziert seit 1998 wissenschaftliche Arbeiten von Studenten, Hochschullehrern und anderen Akademikern als eBook und gedrucktes Buch. Die Verlagswebsite www.grin.com ist die ideale Plattform zur Veröffentlichung von Hausarbeiten, Abschlussarbeiten, wissenschaftlichen Aufsätzen, Dissertationen und Fachbüchern.

Visit us on the internet:

http://www.grin.com/

http://www.facebook.com/grincom

http://www.twitter.com/grin_com

"Heuristics: a source of judgement fallacies or decision-making aids?"

Abstract

This review essay explores different perspectives and conceptualizations of the study of heuristics, decision-making rules which operate under constrained time and computation (Kahneman, 2011). Two opposed models of heuristics that assume conditions of bounded rationality, the *heuristics-and-biases* and the *fast-and-frugal* framework, are assessed. Whereas the former evaluates heuristics in terms of logical rationality and postulates that humans exhibit predictable fallacies in judgement, the latter focuses on ecological validity, and suggests that humans possess an adaptive toolbox of evolutionary developed decision-making rules which enable better decision making. Finally, alternative explanations and limitations of existing research programs will be explored, concluding with a demand for a rigorous evaluation of experimental designs as well as outlining conditions for a possible synthesis.

Table of Contents

- ABSTRACT 1
- **1. INTRODUCTION** 3
- **2. APPROACHES TO RATIONALITY** 4
- **3. THE HEURISTICS-AND-BIASES FRAMEWORK** 5
  - 3.1. THE TWO-SYSTEMS VIEW 5
  - 3.2. ACCESSIBILITY AND THE AVAILABILITY HEURISTIC 7
  - 3.3. NEW HEURISTICS 8
    - *3.3.1. A generic heuristic process* 8
    - *3.3.2. Extension of heuristics* 9
    - *3.3.3 How can System 2 override intuitive judgement (System 1)?* 10
  - 3.4. CRITIQUES TO HAB 10
- **4. FAST-AND-FRUGAL HEURISTICS** 12
  - 4.1. SIMILARITIES TO HAB 12
  - 4.2. DIFFERENCES TO HAB 12
    - *4.2.1. Ecological Rationality* 12
    - *4.2.2. Less-is-more* 13
    - *4.2.3. Bias-Variance Dilemma* 14
    - *4.2.4. A predictable model vs. labels* 15
    - *4.2.5. Adaptive Toolbox: Examples of fast-and-frugal heuristics* 16
  - 4.3. CRITIQUES 17
    - *4.3.1. HAB's reply* 17
    - *4.3.2. Questioning the predictive power of FAF* 18
    - *4.3.3. Evans and Over (2010)* 18
- **5. CONCLUSION** 19
  - 5.1. ALTERNATIVE EXPLANATIONS AND LIMITS OF EXISTING RESEARCH 19
  - 5.2. FUTURE DIRECTIONS: A POSSIBLE SYNTHESIS? 21
- **6. REFERENCES** 23

1. Introduction

Since the 1950s, psychologists have argued that humans are incapable of behaving rationally and optimal. Most prominently, Herbert Simon, advocates:

> 'THE THEORY OF RATIONAL ('SENSIBLE') HUMAN BEHAVIOUR HAS BROKEN LOOSE FROM THE ILLUSORY AND EMPIRICALLY UNSUPPORTED NOTION THAT DECIDING RATIONALLY MEANS MAXIMIZING EXPECTED UTILITY.'
> - Herbert A. Simon, cited in Gigerenzer et al (1999)

In the last three decades, the study of bounded rationality has expanded greatly, especially with Kahneman and Tversky's (1974, 1983) research program. Heuristics, of Greek origin ('serving to find out or discover'), have been defined as intuitive 'rules of thumb' or simple strategies to deal with situations where resources are sparse, which all humans are thought to use similarly (Kahneman et al, 1982).

The present review aims to highlight the origins and definitions of heuristics on the basis of the two most dominant models, the *heuristics-and-biases* (HAB in the following) approach and the *fast-and-frugal* (FAF in the following) framework. Starting with underlying epistemological and philosophical assumptions of both approaches, and then continuously moving towards a comparative evaluation of each research group's main arguments, this essay intends to highlight similarities, differences and possible criticisms. In the conclusion, both theoretical frameworks will be conceptualized, and possible integration possibilities as well as a lack of such an integration to date, will be discussed.

2. Approaches to rationality

In order to discuss the nature of heuristics, it is necessary to highlight different models and assumptions of rationality, which underlie the understanding of human decision-making (Marewski et al, 2010).

Models of <u>unbounded rationality</u> ask how people would behave if they were omniscient (capacity to know everything infinitely) and omnipotent (unlimited power) and assume that decision makers act as if they collect and evaluate all information to reach the mathematically optimal solution. This view is common in the studies of economics and assumes that human decision-making is infinitely flexible and domain-general (Payne et al, 1993).

Models of <u>bounded rationality</u> revise the assumption of rational decision-makers, accounting for the fact that perfectly rational decisions are often not feasible in practice due to finite computational resources available for making them (Simon, 1956). The process of 'satisficing', seeking what is satisfactory rather than optimal, illustrates where behaviour deviates from the tenets of unbounded rationality (Simon, 1957). Where resources are sparse, individuals may employ simple strategies such as heuristics (Simon, 1978). In the following, two approaches to bounded rationality will be discussed.

3. The heuristics-and-biases framework

Since their ground-breaking publication in 'Nature', Kahneman and Tversky (1974) advocated the view that individuals rely on a limited number of heuristic principles when engaging in complex tasks. Although useful by reducing task complexity, these sometimes lead to severe and systematic errors.

In order to evaluate HAB, main assumptions and arguments of its' underlying framework will be examined, before introducing other, more critical perspectives.

3.1. The two-systems view

Kahneman (2002) proposed that intuitive judgements occupy a position between the automatic perception and deliberate operations of reasoning. This distinction between intuition and reasoning, two types of cognitive processes, has been labelled System 1 and 2 (Stanovich & West, 2000).

It is hypothesized that <u>System 1</u> operates automatically, quickly, with little effort, and no sense of voluntary control (Evans & Over, 2010). Similar to the features of perceptual processes, operations are associative, relatively flexible and potentially rule-governed (Petty & Cacioppo, 1986). A picture of an angry woman, for example, automatically evokes certain predispositions about the future (see Figure 1), such as the impression she may say unkind words in a loud voice (Kahneman, 2011).

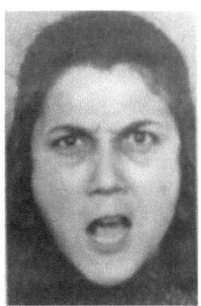

Figure 1: A picture of an angry woman (adapted from Kahneman, 2011)

System 2, on the other hand, deliberately processes information and allocates attention to effortful mental activities. It is involved in all judgements, whether they originate in impressions of System 1 or deliberate reasoning. Moreover, it monitors the quality of both mental operations and overt behaviour (Gilbert, 2002). Therefore, when presented with a multiplication problem (see Figure 2), a precise solution does not easily come to mind. In order to solve this equation, System 2 must be engaged in an effortful and slower thought process.

$$17 \times 24 = ?$$

Figure 2: A multiplication problem (adapted from Kahneman, 2011)

Intuitive answers to judgemental problems proposed by System 1 are monitored by System 2, which makes the explicit judgement and, through monitoring of these proposals, may endorse, correct or override them. However, monitoring is usually quite lax and allows the expression of many intuitive judgements, including some erroneous one's. In one exemplary experiment, Kahneman (2003) posed the following question:

A BAT AND A BALL COST $1.10 IN TOTAL. THE BAT COSTS $1 MORE THAN THE BALL. HOW MUCH DOES THE BALL COST?

Over 50% of participants (students at Princeton University) responded erroneously (0.10$ instead of 0.05$), which illustrates how lightly the output of system 1 (which proposed the wrong answer of 0.10$) is monitored by system 2 (which, had it been utilized, would have calculated the correct answer). Moreover, complex cognitive operations can eventually migrate from system 2 to system 1 as proficiency and skill are acquired (Kahneman & Frederick, 2002), for example the ability of chess masters to instantly perceive the strength or weaknesses of chess positions.

3.2. Accessibility and the availability heuristic

According to HAB, judgements of frequency are made on the basis of item accessibility, a System 1 heuristic, which is replaced by a focus on content when System 2 is more engaged. The ease with which particular mental concepts come to mind (Higgins, 1996) operates on the notion that 'if you can think of it, it must be important' (Esgate & Groom, 2004). To comprehend the workings of System 1, it is important to understand why some thoughts are more accessible than others. For example, the average length of lines in Figure 3 is more easily accessible than the total length of lines.

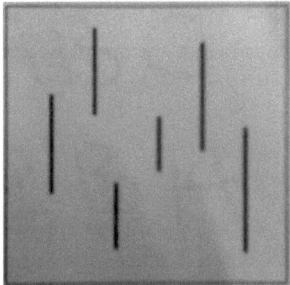

Figure 3: vertical lines of different lengths (adapted from Kahneman, 2002)

Consequently, some attributes seem to be more accessible. These so-called 'natural assessments' are routinely and automatically registered by the perceptual system without intention or effort. Conversely, accessibility is by no means representative of probability, and so heuristics lead to biases and erroneous judgements (Tversky & Kahneman, 1983).

3.3. New Heuristics

Tversky and Kahneman's original theory (1974, 1983) included three heuristics of judgement: representativeness (judgements influenced by what is typical), availability (judgements based on what comes easily to mind) and anchoring (judgements relying on what comes first). The updated model of heuristics proposed by Kahneman and Frederick (2002) departs from the original formulation in three ways:

1. A common process of attribute substitution explains how heuristics work.
2. Extension of the concept of heuristics beyond the domain of judgements about uncertain events.
3. An explicit treatment of the conditions under which intuitive judgements will be modified or overridden by the monitoring operations associated with System 2.

3.3.1. A generic heuristic process

Attribute substitution describes the process of substitution of a specific attribute of a judged object with a related one that comes to mind more easily (i.e. is more readily accessible) as a means to reduce effort. Therefore, when confronted with a difficult question, an easier one may be answered instead outside of conscious awareness (Gilovic et al, 2002). Because the target attribute and the heuristic attribute are different, the substitution of one for the other inevitably introduces systematic biases, where humans violate a law of logic, probability or another standard of rationality. Hence, respondents to a difficult problem offer a reasonable answer to a question they have not been asked. For example, a survey of German students included the following two questions (Kahneman, 2011):

> HOW HAPPY ARE YOU THESE DAYS?
> HOW MANY DATES DID YOU HAVE LAST MONTH?

When phrased in this order, the correlation between the answers was near zero. Evidently, dating was not what came to mind when asked to assess happiness. When another group of students saw the same two questions in reverse order, the correlation between the number of dates and reported happiness was very high. In the first version, dating was apparently not the centre of these student's lives. In the second version, however, evaluations of their romantic life evoked an emotional reaction. Students who had many dates were reminded of a happy aspect of their life, while those who had none were reminded of loneliness and rejection. The emotional aroused by the dating question was still salient when general happiness was queried, and System 1 provided the most accessible answer.

Kahneman (2003) argues that attribute substitution will control judgement when three conditions are satisfied:
1. The target attribute is relatively inaccessible.
2. A semantically and associatively related candidate attribute is highly accessible (such as the 'natural assessments' mentioned above).
3. The substitution is not rejected by system 2 (see below).

3.3.2. Extension of heuristics

Research in the HAB framework has extended the concept of heuristics beyond the domain of judgements about uncertain events, proposing a wide range of heuristics employed by humans leading to predictable biases, such as:

- Anchoring: a particular value for an unknown quantity is being considered before estimating that quantity; estimates stay close to the number considered.
- Framing effects: logically equivalent statements evoke different reactions based on the formulation of beliefs and preferences.
- Prospect Theory: defining outcomes as gains and losses and not as states of wealth has shown that humans evaluate relative to a neutral reference point, following the principle of diminishing sensitivity and loss aversion.

Many more fallacies have been researched as part of the HAB programme, further developing the argument that bounded rationality and the employment of heuristics leads to predictable biases.

3.3.3 How can System 2 override intuitive judgement (System 1)?

Advocates of HAB suggest that the judgements of the intuitive decision-making system can be controlled through the accessibility of corrective thoughts of System 2. Errors of intuitive judgement involve failures of both systems – System 1 that generated the error and System 2 which failed to detect and correct it (Tversky & Kahneman, 1982). What becomes accessible in any particular situation is mainly determined by the actual object of judgement as well as its physical salience (a working of System 1), which can be overcome through deliberate attention (System 2). Research has shown that the efficacy of System 2 is impaired by a wide range of influences, such as time pressure (Finucane et al, 2000), concurrent involvement in a different cognitive task (Gilbert, 2002) and good mood (Isen et al, 1988). Through manipulation of these influences as well as deliberate reasoning, fallacies of intuitive judgements can be overcome and accurate decisions made (Tversky & Kahneman, 1982).

3.4. Critiques to HAB

The main criticisms to HAB stem from a group of researchers collaborating in the 'Centre for Adaptive Behaviour and Cognition' (ABC henceforth), who propose that heuristics are evolutionary adaptations of decision-making processes to specific environments.

Firstly, on an empirical level, ABC criticizes that some of the biases identified by HAB are unstable (Vranas, 2000). The employment of heuristics has been shown to lead to varying consequences amongst different people, thus weakening a general framework view. For example, the magnitude of biases can be reduced significantly by framing research questions differently (e.g. in terms of frequency instead of probability).

Secondly, the ABC argues that HAB generates the misconception that the use of heuristics is always second-best and utilized due to cognitive limitations. Based on the accuracy-effort trade-off, advocates of HAB assume that more information, computation and time would always lead to better results. Contrary to this assumption, research has shown that less information and computation can sometimes lead to higher accuracy in ecologically valid situations. Heuristics can be more accurate than complex procedures, successfully exploiting evolved mental abilities and information available in the environment (Gigerenzer, 2008).

Of central importance is the view of rationality employed by both perspectives. On the one hand, HAB defines and evaluates human decision-making on the basis of principles of probability and logic ('logical rationality'). The ABC, on the other hand, argues that heuristics should be evaluated in terms of ecological rationality, analysing in which environment a given strategy holds or fails (Gigerenzer & Goldstein, 2011). Following this perspective, HAB investigates when heuristics fail and produce biases, whereas the ABC aims to investigate in which environments heuristics hold and produce meaningful results. On a normative level, it may be inaccurate to describe some of the biases identified by HAB as 'errors' in judgement, as no heuristic rule is (ir-)rational per se. Rather than evaluating short-term success on experiments (as HAB does), ABC focuses on a long-term evolutionary perspective.

On a methodological level, Gigerenzer and Goldstein (2011) criticize HAB for assigning vague labels and not producing a precise and testable model, which would make an evaluation of the predictions of heuristics possible. For example, two biases of HAB, the 'Gambler's fallacy' (a base-rate neglect), commonly attributed to the representativeness heuristic, is contrary to the 'hot-hand fallacy' (overweighting the base-rate), easily explained by anchoring on the base rate and adjustment (Gigerenzer & Murray, 1987). No unitary model of heuristics based on HAB can logically account for both, and without the inclusion of a moderator (such as emotions), a distinction is not possible.

4. Fast-and-frugal heuristics

The FAF framework assumes that much of human reasoning and decision-making can be modelled by an adaptive toolbox of simple decision strategies (called heuristics) which are fast and frugal in nature (Marewski et al, 2010). By being tuned to regularities in the structure of the task environment and exploiting the ways in which basic cognitive capacities work, each heuristic employs a minimum of time, knowledge and computation (Gigerenzer et al, 1999). In contrast to HAB, FAF does not view heuristics as simplified versions of complex rational strategies (Heukelom, 2005).

The ABC programme has two interrelated components (Hutchinson & Gigerenzer, 2005); first, to demonstrate in which environments a given heuristic performs well ('ecological rationality'); secondly, to study the heuristics that people actually use ('adaptive toolbox').

4.1. Similarities to HAB

Both HAB and FAF postulate that norms and predictions of classical theories of rationality are systematically violated by human decision makers in a variety of specific ways, where decisions are better accounted for in terms of various heuristics (Gigerenzer & Goldstein, 2011). Moreover, both HAB and FAF are concerned with finding the situations in which heuristics are utilized (Gigerenzer et al, 1999).

4.2. Differences to HAB

4.2.1. Ecological Rationality

A fundamental differentiation between HAB and FAF is their view of rationality. As outlined above, HAB focuses on 'logical rationality' and views heuristics as inferior to deliberate decision-making, basing claims of fallacies and biases on a violation of logical rules (Gilovic et al, 2002).

FAF, on the other hand, focuses on the correspondence-based performance of heuristics in real-world environments. ABC uses the term 'heuristic' in the same positive sense as earlier researchers (Simon & Newell, 1958), emphasizing its beneficial role. What matters to ABC is the performance of heuristics in real environments and the way the human mind can take advantage of the structure of information in the environment to arrive at reasonable decisions, because many so-called 'biases' are actually evolutionary adaptive (Gigerenzer, 2000). Researchers of FAF believe that heuristics can be faster, more frugal and more accurate at the same time, both in theory and in practice.

4.2.2. Less-is-more

Researchers in the FAF framework maintain that the general accuracy-effort trade-off does not always hold. These so-called 'less-is-more' effects, where more information and computation can actually decrease accuracy, provides the rationale for concluding that minds rely on simple heuristics in order to be more accurate (Gigerenzer & Brighton, 2009). Even if direct and opportunity costs were zero, the mind would not gain anything from relying on complex strategies. Instead, Hutchinson and Gigerenzer (2005) argue, heuristics exploit evolved abilities, such as recognition memory ('recognition heuristic'), recollection memory ('take-the-best' heuristic.) and object-tracking ('ball-catching' heuristic). It is important to note that FAF does not challenge the ability to perform deliberate decision-making, but questions whether this is necessary and adaptive for routine decisions (Hutchinson & Gigerenzer, 2005). For example, Beilock et al (2004) found that expert golfers, but not novices, perform better under constrained versus unconstrained time.

In sum, the less-is-more effect forces a reassessment of normative ideals of rationality and provides evidence for an ecological rather than a logical rationality.

4.2.3. Bias-Variance Dilemma

Both HAB and FAF believe that heuristics lead to biases but differ in their understandings of their outcome. For FAF, a biased algorithm produced by a heuristic can be more accurate than an unbiased one. As an example, Gigerenzer (2008) analyses London's temperature in 2000, and computes the average temperature of each day, establishing patterns through the use of varying degrees of polynomials. As can be seen in Figure 4, higher degrees of polynomials increase the fit; 'degree 12 polynomial' offers a closer fit to observed temperatures compared to 'degree 3 polynomial'.

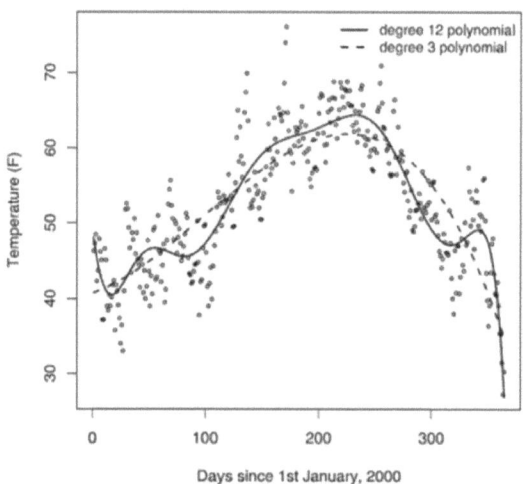

Figure 4: polynomial curves of London's daily temperatures in 2000 (from Gigerenzer, 2011)

However, when it comes to predicting outcomes, complex models using a high degree of polynomials are more likely to contain error, which shows that too much complexity leads to unrealistic models. Decomposing error into the sum of its three components bias, variance and noise, Gigerenzer and Brighton (2009) found that, as models become more complex (i.e. more polynomials), bias falls, whereas variance increases (see Figure 5).

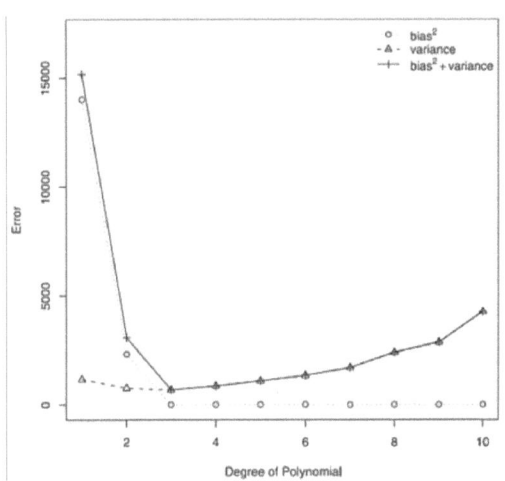

Figure 5: Total Error, decomposed for bias and variance (from Gigerenzer, 2011)

This fundamental problem in statistical inferences, known as the bias-variance dilemma, shows that in order to achieve low prediction error, a model must accommodate a vast variety of patterns in order to ensure low bias. This variety that a model must accommodate however, is likely to come with an increase in variance, thus diminishing the models' usefulness. Therefore, a reliance on 'biased' heuristics allows handling uncertainty more efficiently and robustly than more resource-intensive and general-purpose strategies leading to better predictions than unbiased one's (Geman et al, 1992).

4.2.4. A predictable model vs. labels

Built on the ABC's critique of HAB for using vague labels, FAF opts for a model of heuristics, which specifies the precise steps of information gathering and processing involved in generating a decision (Gigerenzer et al, 1999). These include specific principles for (a) guiding a search for alternatives, information or both, (b) stopping that search and (c) making a decision. On the basis of constructed computational models, it is possible to mathematically evaluate the predictions made by FAF and test for the validity of individual heuristics.

4.2.5. Adaptive Toolbox: Examples of fast-and-frugal heuristics

As previously outlined, the FAF approach hypothesizes that the human mind consists of a number of evolved strategies, which constitute the building blocks of fast-and-frugal heuristics. These heuristic adaptive strategies of the adaptive toolbox are domain or context specific and can be used as building blocks to develop new decision-making strategies depending on the environmental conditions (Gigerenzer et al, 1999). Examples of heuristics in the adaptive toolbox include:

- recognition: the use of familiarity as a probabilistic cue. When asked to identify the larger of two cities, Gigerenzer and Hoffrage (1995) found that German students were more accurate on a sample of American rather than German cities. The lack of recognition of one of the two presented American cities was used as information, inferring that the recognized city is larger. For German cities, German students knew too much and could not rely on the recognition heuristic.
- fluency: use of the ease of retrieval as a cue for higher value (Schooler & Hertwig, 2005).
- 'take-the-best': consists of a three-step approach in order to infer which of two alternatives has the higher value: First, cues are searched in order of validity; secondly, the search is stopped as soon as a cue discriminates both options; lastly, the cue favoured by the alternative is chosen (Gigerenzer & Goldstein, 2011) The predictive accuracy exceeded that of other models (Gigerenzer & Brighton, 2009).

There are numerous other heuristics identified by FAF, further making the point that the adaptive toolbox contains the building blocks for many decision-making strategies.

4.3. Critiques

4.3.1. HAB's reply

Due to the nature of their research, the HAB approach is fundamentally opposed to claims of the FAF framework, to the extent that both research programs have adopted an antagonistic stance towards each other:

> 'IT IS NOT UNCOMMON IN ACADEMIC DEBATES THAT A CRITIC'S DESCRIPTION OF THE OPPONENT'S IDEAS AND FINDINGS INVOLVES SOME LOSS OF FIDELITY [...]. IN SOME EXCEPTIONAL CASES, HOWEVER, THE FIDELITY OF THE PRESENTATION IS SO LOW THAT READERS MAY BE MISLED ABOUT THE REAL ISSUES UNDER DISCUSSION. IN OUR VIEW, GIGERENZER'S CRITIQUE OF THE HEURISTICS AND BIASES PROGRAM IS ONE OF THESE CASES.'
>
> - Tversky and Kahneman (1996)

Contrary to Gigerenzer et al's (1988) claim that HAB is 'independent of context and content', Kahneman and Tversky (1996) argue that framing effects, where different framings of the same problem or judgement give rise to different results, show that HAB acknowledges sensitivity to different representations of problems.

Furthermore, Gigerenzer (1991) asserts that, under certain conditions, heuristic fallacies, such as the base-rate neglect, disappear. Critiques, such as Camerer (1990), show that underweighting of base-rate has been demonstrated in several studies, even when participants drew random samples from a specified sample. Naturally, there are conditions under which the correct answer is transparent, for example when the two figures in the Müller-Lyer illusion are embedded in a rectangular frame. However, this observation does not make the illusion less interesting (Kahneman & Tversky, 1996).

Moreover, FAF criticizes HAB for not providing a formal definition of heuristics, stating that they are 'largely undefined concepts and can post-hoc be used to explain almost everything' (Gigerenzer et al, 1991). Kahneman and

Tversky (1996) suggest that this objection fails to recognize that representativeness can be assessed experimentally. Therefore, it need not be defined a priori, as testing the hypothesis that probability judgments are mediated by representativeness does not require a theoretical model.

Opposing Gigerenzer's argument that HAB is 'narrowly Bayesian', Tversky and Kahneman (1996) argue that the refusal to apply the concept of probability to unique events is a fallacy in FAF. Subjective probabilities are not meaningless (as even the ABC has used this source of data), but by denying normative standards to these judgments, the ABC invokes normative agnosticism, which is unreasonably permissive. As Tversky and Kahneman (1996) propose, for example, 'is it not a mistake for a speaker to assign probabilities of .99 both to an event and to its complement?'. Such a fallacy of subjective probability estimation cannot be disregarded.

4.3.2. Questioning the predictive power of FAF

Newell et al (2003) question the predictive power of fast-and-frugal heuristics. In their decision-making test, only 33% of participants behaved in a manner consistent with the 'take-the-best' heuristic, with the majority adopting a non-frugal strategy accumulating far more information than predicted. A meta-analysis of 136 studies in which human judgment was compared to algorithmic prediction found that 63 studies discovered an advantage for algorithms, versus just 8 which found the opposite (Grove et al, 2000). In sum, fast-and-frugal heuristic do not seem to be as accurate as suggested.

4.3.3. Evans and Over (2010)

Three additional criticisms of FAF have been proposed by Evans and Over (2010). Firstly, using the fluency heuristics as an example, they argue that aspects of the retrieval process and not the accessibility of memories per se may give rise to metacognitive cues (Koriat, 1993). Thus, feelings can be false cues and lead to judgment fallacies.

Secondly, Evans and Over (2010) emphasize the importance of logic in heuristics. FAF claims that the 'adaptive toolbox' has a trustworthy 'sort of instinct' (Gigerenzer & Hoffrage, 1995). Nonetheless, there are some instances where it is necessary to follow laws of logic and probability, which can be frugal as well (Kleiter, 1994).

Lastly, Evans and Over (2010) emphasize the importance of the dual-process theory (Stanovich & West, 2000), which has been entirely ignored by advocates of FAF. The evidence for two separate cognitive processes has been accumulating over the past 40 years, and the insights gathered provide a rational and useful value of heuristics.

5. Conclusion

5.1. Alternative Explanations and limits of existing research

This review on the topic of heuristics brought together various perspectives, aiming to give a complete account of all major frameworks presently being discussed in the area. To date, it is being heatedly debated whether heuristics are a source of judgement fallacies (HAB) or decision-making aids (FAF). Besides many commonalities, there are several fundamental disjunctions between both approaches.

On a philosophical level, although generally accepting that the employment of heuristics occurs in a setting where information in the environment is limited, HAB believes that more information and computation would lead to more accurate results, whereas FAF states that because heuristics are evolutionary adaptations to specific task environments, their use will lead to more accurate results. On an epistemological level, researchers in the HAB domain study where task performance breaks down and leads to predictable biases, employing a short-term, accuracy focussed view. Advocates of FAF emphasize the long-term development and application of heuristics in realistic environments, and therefore investigate where heuristics lead to better task performance utilizing mathematical models, exemplarily illustrated with the bias-variance dilemma. Due to the adverse relationships of researchers associating with either perspective, there have been little critical evaluations of the methodology of experiments utilized by either framework. Instead, both HAB and FAF develop their own arguments within their respective research program, without response, reference or referral to the work of researchers of the other approach, making an assessment as to which of the discussed theories contains most validity difficult.

Theoretical drawbacks are often highlighted by researchers of other domains, such as studies by experimental economists, who have criticized the artificial laboratory conditions utilized by both approaches. Many postulations of both frameworks do not hold when circumstances are varied (Plott & Zeiler, 2005/2007). Additionally, both HAB and FAF claim that subjects facing hypothetical choices can imagine how they would actually behave under high incentive conditions. This assertion has been questioned by Holt and Laury (2002, 2005) who were able to demonstrate that behaviour can be dramatically different when real instead of hypothetical incentives are used. Economists stress the fact that researchers studying heuristics must address these shortcomings prior to criticizing economics for its assumption of unbounded rationality (Harrison et al, 2005).

Although the differentiations between HAB and FAF are so profound, Shah and Oppenheimer (2009) intend to combine both frameworks. Building on Simon's (1990) definition of heuristics as 'methods for arriving at satisfactory solutions with modest amounts of computations', their main focus is on the potential of heuristics to reduce effort exerted in limited-information environments. Shah and Oppenheimer (2008) aim to find common ground by identification of the great redundancy within both approaches, deemphasizing the exaggerated focus on domain-specific heuristics and by focussing research on the methods underlying decision-making processes. As Hammond (1990) points out, research should do more than 'offer a list of heuristics that have been demonstrated to occur under conditions created to demonstrate them'. Far from being accepted equally by researchers in both fields, Gigerenzer and Brighton

(2009) argue that accuracy-effort trade-offs are the conventional justifications for why the cognitive system relies on heuristics, ignoring the challenges made by the less-is-more effect proposed by FAF. Hence, contrary to its objective, Gigerenzer and Brighton (2009) locate this 'effort-reduction framework' within the HAB domain, continuing the divide between both research groups.

Regardless of the debate on heuristics, their wider importance is gradually being acknowledged. Although mostly lacking application, legislation is sparingly evolving which aims to navigate people towards better judgements by presenting choices in different ways. Thus, for a example, a new British legislation, taking into account HAB's framing effects, changes the default option for corporate pension plans, whereby employees are automatically enrolled unless they actively choose to opt out (Depczyk, 2012).

5.2. Future Directions: A possible synthesis?

It is the contention of this essay to illustrate that the only possible way to reach a resolution between researchers studying heuristics is through a rigorous evaluation of experimental designs and procedures utilized by each research group. As experimental economists have pointed out, neither approach is without flaws, and both frameworks must acknowledge that taken alone, neither is sufficient.

One possible avenue for a synthesis would be to place both approaches to the study of heuristics on a unified timescale. In the short-term, an individual's use of heuristics may lead to biases (as is the argument of HAB), whereby taking more time and information into account will lead to more accurate judgements. However, in the long-term, heuristics have evolved as evolutionary adaptive strategies (as is the argument of FAF), which in general lead to more accurate results in situations where more time and information is simply not available. In the long run, biases may enable a higher predictive accuracy of strategies when less information is used.

Utilizing this point of view, both approaches are seemingly integratable, as epistemological and philosophical differences are attributed to different time perspectives. For a more widespread application of research insights, it is imperative to address the shortcomings highlighted by experimental economists, which can be addressed more efficiently by incorporating both perspectives into a unified model. With the addition of time as a continuous variable, it is possible for both approaches to set their differences aside and combine research efforts.

6. References

Becker, G.S. (1962). Irrational Behaviour and Economic Theory. *The Journal of Political Economy*, *70*(1), 1-13

Beilock, S.L., Berthenthal, B.I., Mccoy, A.M., Carr, T.H. (2004). Haste does not always make waste: Expertise, direction of attention and speed versus accuracy in performing sensorimotor skills. *Psychonomic Bulleting & Review*, *11*(2), 373-379

Berg, N., Gigerenzer, G (2010). As-if behavioral economics: Neoclassical economics in disguise? *Published in: History of Economic Ideas*, *18*(1), 133-166

Camerer, C. (1990). Do markets correct biases in probability judgment? Evidence from market experiments. *Advances in behavioral economics, 2*, 126-172

Colander, D., Föllmer, H., Haas, A., Goldberg, M., Juselius, K., Kirman, A., Lux, T., Sloth, B. (2009). The financial crisis and the systematic failure of academic economics. *Groupement de Recherche en Economie*

Coursey, D.L., Hovis, J.L., Schulze, W.D. (1987). The Disparity Between Willingness to Accept and Willingness to Pay Measures of Value. *The Quarterly Journal of Economics*, *102*(3), 679-690.

Depczyk, J. (2012, March 24). Nudge nudge, think think. *The Economist*. Retrieved April 14, 2012, from http://www.economist.com/node/21551032

Esgate, A.; Groome, D. (2004). *An Introduction to Applied Cognitive Psychology*. New York: Psychology Press.

Evans, J., Over, D.E. (2010). Heuristic thinking and human intelligence: a commentary on Marewski, Gaissmaier and Gigerenzer. *Cogn Process, 11,* 171-175

Finucane, M. L. Alhakami, A. Slovic, P. Johnson, S. M. (2000). The Affect Heuristic in Judgments of Risks and Benefits. *Journal of behavioural decision making*, 13(1), 1-18

Geman, S., Bienenstock, E., Doursat, R. (1992). Neural Networks and the Bias/Variance Dilemma. *Neural Computation*, 4(1), 1-58

Gigerenzer, G., Murray, D.J. (1987). *Cognition as intuitive statistics.* Hillsdale, NJ: Lawrence Erlbaum Associates.

Gigerenzer, G., Hell, W., & Blank, H. (1988). Presentation and content: The use of base rates as a continuous variable. *Journal of Experimental Psychology: Human Perception and Performance, 14,* 513-525.

Gigerenzer, G. (1991). How to make cognitive illusions disappear: Beyond "heuristics and biases." *European review of social psychology, 2,* 83-115

Gigerenzer, G., Hoffrage, U. (1995). How to improve Bayesian reasoning without instruction: Frequency formats. *Psychological Review, 102*(4), 684-704.

Gigerenzer, G. (1996). On Narrow Terms and Vague Heuristics: A Reply to Kahneman and Tversky (1996). *Psychological Review, 103*(2), 592-596

Gigerenzer, G., Todd, P. M., & ABC Research Group (1999). *Simple Heuristics That Make Us Smart.* Oxford: Oxford University Press.

Gigerenzer, G. (2000). *Adaptive Thinking : rationality in the real world.* New York: Oxford University Press.

Gigerenzer, G., Selten, R. (2002). *Bounded Rationality: The Adaptive Toolbox*. London: MIT Press.

Gigerenzer, G. (2008). Why Heuristics Work. *Perspectives on Psychological Science, 3*(1), 20-29

Gigerenzer, G., Brighton, H. (2009), Homo Heuristicus: Why Biased Minds Make Better Inferences. *Topics in Cognitive Science, 1*, 107–143

Gigerenzer, G., Goldstein, D.G. (2011a). The recognition heuristic: A decade of research. *Judgment and Decision Making, 6*(1), 100-121

Gigerenzer, G. (2011, April 11th). *For faster and better decisions, a biased and less-informed mind.* Presentation at Behavioural Science Institute, Singapore Management University

Gilbert, D. T. (2002). Inferential correction. In T. Gilovich, D. Griffin & D. Kahneman (Eds.), Heuristics and biases (pp.167–184). New York: Cambridge University Press.

Gilovich, T., Griffin, D., & Kahneman, D. (Eds.). (2002). Heuristics and Biases. New York: Cambridge University Press.

Grove, W.M., Zald, D.H. Lebow, B.S., Snitz. B.E., Nelson, C. (2000). Clinical versus mechanical prediction: A meta-analysis. *Psychological Assessment, 12*(1), 19-30

Hammond, K. R. (1990). Functionalism and illusionism: Can integration be usefully achieved? In R. M. Hogarth (Ed.), *Insights in decision making: A tribute to Hillel J. Einhorn.* Chicago: University of Chicago.

Harford, T. (2011, January 28). Why we do what we do. *Financial Times*. Retrieved from: http://www.ft.com/

Harrison, G.W., Johnson, E., McInnes, M.M., Rutstrom, E.E. (2005). Risk Aversion and Incentive Effect: Comment. *American Economic Review*, 95(3), 897-901

Heukelom, F. (2005). Gigerenzer the Decided. *Tinbergen Institute Discussion Paper, 113/2*

Higgins, E.T. (1996). Knowledge activation: Accessibility, applicability, and salience. Social psychology: Handbook of basic principles. In: *Social psychology: Handbook of basic principles*. Higgins, E.T., Kruglanski, A.W. (Eds.), New York: Guilford Press.

Holt, C.A., Laury, S.K. (2002). Risk Aversion and Incentive Effect. *American Economic Review, 92(5)*, 1644-1655

Holt, C.A., Laury, S.K. (2005). Risk Aversion and Incentive Effect: New Data without Order Effects. *American Economic Review, 95(3)*, 902-904

Hurley, S. (2005). Social heursitics that make us smarter. *Philosophical Psychology, 18(5)*, 585-612

Hutchinson, J.M.C., Gigerenzer, G. (2005). Simple heuristics and rules of thumb: Where psychologists and behavioural biologists might meet. *Behavioural Processes, 69(2)*, 97-124

Isen, A.M., Nygren, T.E., Ashby, F.G. (1988). Influence of positive affect on the subjective utility of gains and losses: It is just not worth the risk. *Journal of Personality and Social Psychology, 55(5)*, 710-717

Isoni, A., Loomes, G., Sugden, R. (2009). The Willingness to Pay-Willingness to Accept Gap, the "Endowment Effect", Subject Misconceptions, and Experimental Procedures for Eliciting Valuations: Replication and Reassessment.

Jacoby, L.L., Dallas, M. (1981). On the relationship between autobiographical memory and perceptual learning. *Journal of Experimental Psychology*, *110*(3), 306-340.

Kahneman, D., Slovic, P., Tversky, A. (1982). *Judgment under Uncertainty: Heuristics and Biases*. Cambridge: Cambridge University Press

Kahneman, D., Tversky, A. (1984). Choices, values, and frames. *American Psychologist*, *39*(4), 341-350.

Kahneman, D., Knetsch, J. L., Thaler, R.H. (1990a). Experimental Tests of the Endowment Effect and the Coase Theorem. *Journal of Political Economy*, *98*(6), 1325-1348.

Kahneman, D., Knetsch, J. L., Thaler, R.H. (1991). The Endowment Effect, Loss Aversion, and Status Quo Bias. *Journal of Economic Perspectives, 5*(1), 193-206.

Kahneman, D., Tversky, T. (1996). On the Reality of Cognitive Illusions. *Psychological Review*, *103*(2), 582-591

Kahneman, D., Frederick, S. (2002). Representativeness revisited: Attribute substitution in intuitive judgment. In: *Heuristics and biases: The psychology of intuitive judgements*, Gilovic, T, Griffin, D., Kahneman, D (Eds.), New York : Cambridge University Press

Kahneman, D. (2003a). Maps of Bounded Rationality: Psychology for Behavioral Economics, *American Economic Review, 93*(5), 1449-1475

Kahneman, D. (2003b). A perspective on judgment and choice: Mapping bounded rationality. *American Psychologist, 58*(9), 697-720

Kahneman, D. (2011). *Thinking, fast and slow*. London: Allen Lane

Khader, P.H., Pachur, T., Meier, S., Bien, S., Jost, K., Rösler, F. (2011). Memory-based Decision-making with Heuristics: Evidence for a Controlled Activation of Memory Representations. *Journal of Cognitive Neuroscience, 23*(11), 3540-3554

Loewenstein, G., Ubel, P. (2010, July 14). Economics Behaving Badly. *New York Times*. Retrieved from: http://www.nytimes.com/

Marewski, J.N., Gaissmaier, W., Gigerenzer, G. (2010). Good judgments do not require complex cognition. *Cognitive Processing, 11*(2), 103-121

Newell, B.R., Weston, N.J., Shanks, D.R. (2003). Empirical Tests of a fast-and-frugal heuristic: Not everyone takes "take-the-best". *Organizational Behaviour and Human Decision Processes, 91*(1), 82-96

Oppenheimer, D.M. (2003). Not so fast! (and not so frugal!): rethinking the recognition heuristic. *Cognition*. Volume 90. B1-B9.

Payne, J.W., Bettman, J.R., Eric, J. (1993). *The adaptive decision maker*. New York : Cambridge University Press

Petty, R.E., Cacioppo, J.T. (1986). *Communication and persuasion: Central and peripheral routes to attitude change.* New York: Springer-Verlag

Pinker, S. (1997). *How the mind works.* New York: W.W. Norton & Company.

Plott, C.R., Zeiler, K (2007). Exchange Asymmetries Incorrectly Interpreted as Evidence of Endowment Effect Theory and Prospect Theory? *The American Economic Review,* 97(4), 1449-1466.

Schooler, L.J., Hertwig, R. (2005). How Forgetting Aids Heuristic Inference. *Psychological Review, 112*(3), 610-628.

Shah, A.K., Oppenheimer, D.M. (2008). Heuristics Made Easy: An Effort-Reduction Framework. *Psychological Bulletin, 134* (2), 207-222

Shah. A.K., Oppenheimer, D.M. (2009). The Path of Least Resistance. Using Easy-to-Access Information. *Current Directions in Psychological Science, 18*(4), 232-236

Simon, H. A. (1956). Rational choice and the structure of the environment. *Psychological Review, 63*(2), 129-138.

Simon, H. A. (1957). A Behavioral Model of Rational Choice. In Simon, H. A. (Ed.), *Models of Man, Social and Rational: Mathematical Essays on Rational Human Behavior in a Social Setting.* New York: Wiley.

Simon, H.A., Newell, A. (1958). Heuristic Problem Solving: The Next Advance in Operations Research. *Operations Research,* 6(1), 1-10

Simon, H.A. (1978). Rationality as a process and product of thought. *American Economic Review, 89,* 1-16.

Simon, H. A. (1981). *The sciences of the artificial.* Cambridge, MA: MIT Press.

Simon, H. A. (1982). *Models of bounded rationality.* Cambridge, MA: MIT Press.

Simon, H.A. (1983). *Reason in human affairs.* Stanford: Stanford University Press

Simon, H. A. (1990). Invariants of human behavior. *Annual Review of Psychology, 41,* 1-19.

Stanovich, K.E., West, R.F. (2000). Individual differences in reasoning: Implications for the rationality debate?. *Behavioral Brain Science,* 23(5), 645-665

Tversky, A., Kahneman, D. (1971). Belief in the law of small numbers. *Psychological Bulletin, 76*(2), 105-110

Tversky, A., Kahneman, D. (1974). Judgment under Uncertainty: Heuristics and Biases. *Science, 185*(4157), 1124-1131

Tversky, A., Kahneman, D. (1983). Extensional versus intuitive reasoning: The conjunction fallacy in probability judgment. *Psychology Review, 90*(4), 293-315

Vranas, P.B.M. (2000). Gigerenzer's normative critique of Kahneman & Tversky. *Cognition, 76,* 179-193